To

_____

From

_____

Date

_____

Hi friend,

Welcome to a new guided journaling experience. This journal is all about self-discovery and journeying to the places that make you *you*. God has created you in a specific way to carry out the purposes for your life and for others from your unique combination of experience, personality, strengths, and perspectives. If we're not in tune with our own true thoughts, convictions, and values, then it's not long before we find ourselves overwhelmed with life, shapeshifting into the opinions and images of those around us while losing ourselves in the process. So these daily prompts are meant to help you through defining some of the basic, foundational areas that guide your life—while providing some encouragement and tips to renew your mind along the way.

My hope is that through this journaling process you'll be able to:

- Gain a broader sense of self-awareness by being able to see and understand your present thought patterns and emotional state to help you grow.

- Develop healthy habits for your mind, body, and soul.

- Tangibly track your goals, your mental health, your visions, and your dreams.

- In a world full of opinions and perspectives, you can sort out your own voice, values, and convictions and grow into the individual God created you to be.

By gaining clarity in our thoughts and intentions, we can step confidently into our relationships and the life we're called to live, from a place of mental, emotional, and spiritual awareness and purpose. Amen? Enjoy!

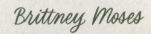

KNOWN

An Inspirational
Journal for
Self-Discovery

Brittney
Moses

DaySpring
LIVE YOUR FAITH

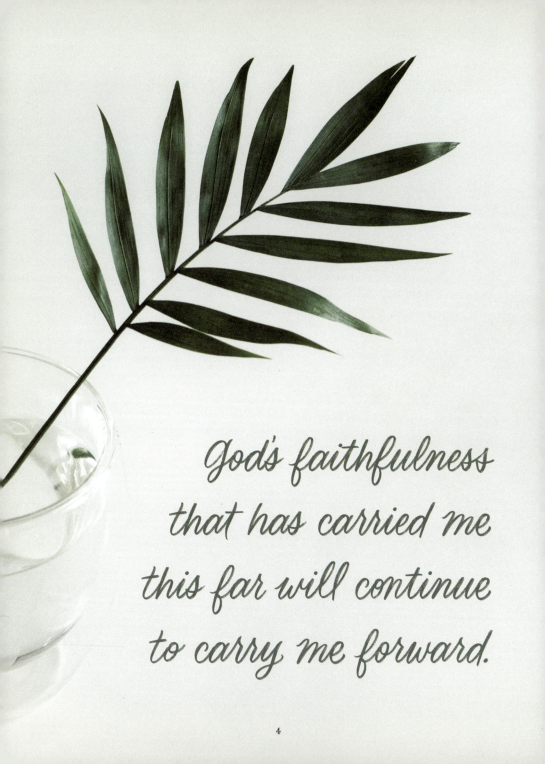

God's faithfulness
that has carried me
this far will continue
to carry me forward.

On a scale of 1–10, how would I currently rate my anxiety, and what can I start doing this week to better protect my mental health?

_____

_____

_____

_____

_____

_____

_____

_____

_____

_____

_____

_____

_____

_____

QUICK TIP:

When you feel overwhelmed, consider shifting from big-picture thinking to smaller-picture thinking and focusing on being present with what you can manage for the day, releasing the stress and letting tomorrow deal with tomorrow (Matthew 6:34). Make a list of the responsibilities that are causing you the most distress; list them from most stressful to least stressful. First deal with your most urgent responsibilities; this will alleviate some space and relief. Then work your way down to less stressful responsibilities over the course of the week.

TODAY I FEEL . . .

My spirit
may grow weak,
but God remains the
strength of my heart.

PSALM 73:26 NLT

What small steps will help me

adjust to current changes in my life?

_____

_____

_____

_____

_____

_____

_____

_____

_____

_____

_____

_____

_____

_____

_____

_____

_____

_____

_____

_____

_____

_____

_____

_____

_____

_____

_____

_____

_____

_____

_____

_____

_____

_____

_____

_____

_____

_____

_____

_____

QUICK TIP:

Remind yourself that life is not about always being in control but about learning how to adapt. The more we try to control the circumstances in our lives, the more anxious we feel when things don't play out the way we pictured. Instead, practice a life of flexibility knowing that God has you no matter the outcome. Ask yourself, "Now that I'm in this situation, what are the next steps I need to take to adapt and move forward?" This is how we grow.

TODAY I'M GRATEFUL FOR . . .

No matter what it looks like . . .
No matter what it feels like . . .
No matter how much it hurts . . .
No matter the anxiety . . .
No matter the depression . . .
No matter the diagnosis . . .
The Lord will fulfill
His purpose for me.

What do I need to let go of

that's out of my control today?

_____
_____
_____
_____
_____
_____
_____
_____
_____
_____
_____
_____
_____
_____
_____
_____
_____
_____
_____
_____
_____
_____
_____
_____
_____
_____

_____

_____

_____

_____

_____

_____

_____

_____

_____

_____

_____

_____

_____

_____

QUICK TIP:

The problem with control fallacies is that we have either bought into the belief that we should be able to control things that we realistically cannot, or we feel hopeless as if we have no control in situations where we can actually take small steps toward change. So, today's challenge is to find the balance between the two. Consider what actions you can take to make progress in the things you can control (even if it's your own attitude and behavior), and release the things that you cannot change so you can be at peace with yourself.

MY PRAYER FOR TODAY IS . . .

You don't have to show up in the way that others show up in order to be worthy.

Write about where you were this time last year

and what you've learned since then.

QUICK TIP:

Instead of shaming yourself over the disappointment of past decisions, consider that you did what you thought was best in the moment, given the information and perspective you had at that point in time. It's not until you know more or have better context that you can grow and do better. So, give yourself grace during this growth process and know that at any point, you are allowed to make a change.

TODAY I HOPE . . .

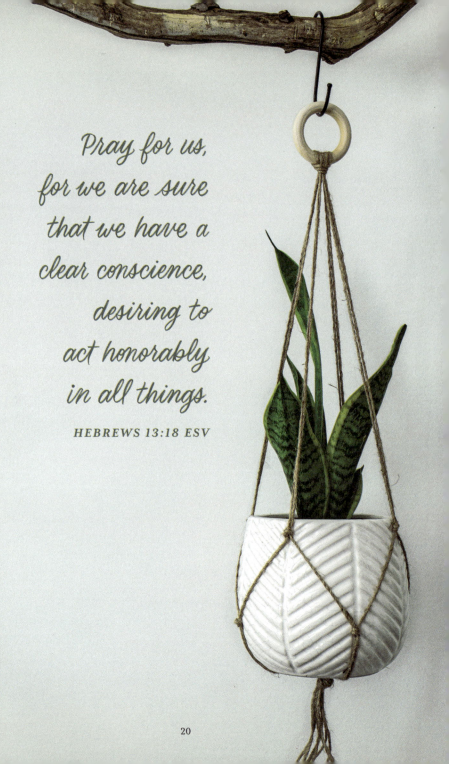

Pray for us,
for we are sure
that we have a
clear conscience,
desiring to
act honorably
in all things.

HEBREWS 13:18 ESV

Five core values that guide my life are . . .

_____

_____

_____

_____

_____

_____

_____

_____

_____

_____

_____

_____

_____

QUICK TIP:

Core values are the principles and ideas that ultimately guide our choices and actions. Oftentimes when we feel anxiety, frustration, or a loss of self, it's because we are experiencing a cognitive dissonance. Our actions are not in alignment with the convictions and values we deeply believe in. Consider in which areas your actions haven't been aligning with your core values and where changes need to be made.

TODAY I FEEL . . .

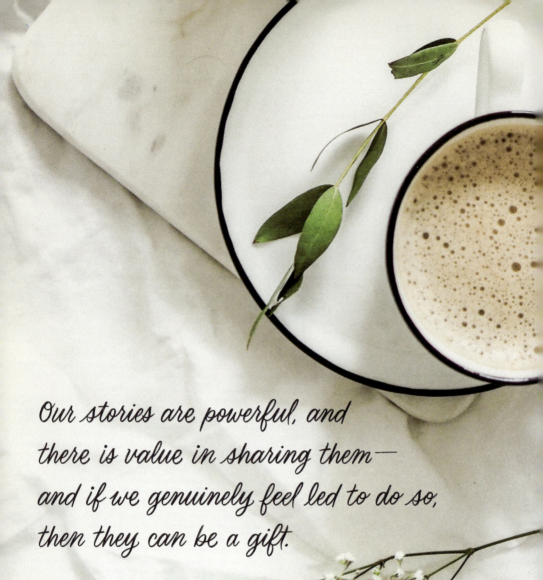

Our stories are powerful, and there is value in sharing them— and if we genuinely feel led to do so, then they can be a gift.

Who are three people I'd like

to call or video this month and why?

_____

_____

_____

_____

_____

_____

_____

_____

_____

_____

_____

_____

_____

_____

_____

_____

QUICK TIP:

When we bond and form healthy attachments with others, neurochemicals like oxytocin and dopamine release in the brain that can make us feel happier and less stressed. This is why social health is also a big component of mental and emotional health. This affirms God's truth that we were not created to do life alone (Genesis 2:18) and two are better than one (Ecclesiastes 4:9–12). Consider making genuine connection a priority in your schedule. Your mental and emotional health will thank you for it!

TODAY I'M GRATEFUL FOR . . .

Nothing can separate
you from God's love.
That's not a feeling—
that's a promise.

What would my ideal morning

and evening routine look like?

_____
_____
_____
_____
_____
_____
_____
_____
_____
_____
_____
_____
_____
_____
_____
_____
_____
_____
_____
_____
_____
_____
_____
_____
_____
_____

_____

_____

_____

_____

_____

_____

_____

_____

_____

_____

_____

_____

_____

_____

_____

QUICK TIP:

Consider visualizing your day. Meditate on how you'd like to move through your day and what that practically looks like for you. For example, think about where you need more focus, more self-control, or better boundaries in certain areas, or how you plan on winding down and finding rest in the evening. While things may not always go as perfectly as you picture them, a visualization practice can help you be better grounded within yourself and become more intentional and less reactive throughout your day.

MY PRAYER FOR TODAY IS . . .

How anxious am I feeling right now?

☐ 1 Slightly worried but functioning as usual   ☐ 2 Mildly growing fear and stress   ☐ 3 Can't focus and obsessive overthinking   ☐ 4 Losing control with physical discomfort   ☐ 5 Nearing anxiety attack

LET IT OUT: *What has happened or is about to happen that's causing my anxiety?*

_____

_____

_____

IDENTIFY: *Why does this scare me? What are my thoughts saying?*

_____

_____

_____

PERSPECTIVE CHANGE: *These are two other ways I could look at the situation . . .*

1. _____

_____

2. _____

_____

Stop. Breathe. Is this outside my control?

IF YES, I CAN NO LONGER CARRY THE BURDEN AND I RELEASE MYSELF FROM THE BONDAGE OF THAT WHICH I HAVE NO CONTROL.

This is the first step I can take to face the situation and overcome my fear:

_____

Who can I talk to or ask for prayer?

_____

Two things I am grateful for in this moment:

1. _____

2. _____

MY GOAL:

TO BE ACHIEVED BY:

The specific steps I need to take:

☐

☐

☐

☐

☐

PRIORITY GOALS FOR THE WEEK	DATE COMPLETED

I'M REWARDING MYSELF FOR FULFILLING MY GOALS BY:

DATE:

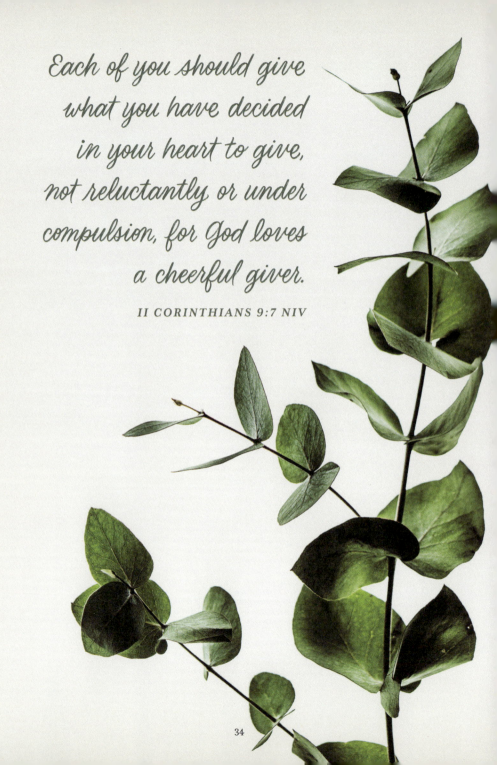

Each of you should give
what you have decided
in your heart to give,
not reluctantly or under
compulsion, for God loves
a cheerful giver.

II CORINTHIANS 9:7 NIV

What boundaries do I need to

better focus on my tasks today?

_____
_____
_____
_____
_____
_____
_____
_____
_____
_____
_____
_____
_____
_____
_____
_____
_____
_____
_____
_____
_____
_____
_____
_____
_____
_____
_____
_____
_____

_____

_____

_____

_____

_____

_____

_____

_____

_____

_____

_____

_____

_____

_____

QUICK TIP:

Second Corinthians 9:7 reminds us that genuine giving is a decision made in our hearts, not out of fear or reactivity. God called us to be people lovers, not people pleasers. When we love, it's from a place of freedom. People-pleasing is rooted in fear and conformity and results in abandoning our true selves and convictions. Whether it be our time, talents, or finances, only we know the context of our own giving capacity. So, there's no shame in drawing healthy boundaries so you can ultimately do what you're called to do as a cheerful giver.

TODAY I HOPE . . .

It's okay if this season means
focusing on your recovery
so you're in a better position
mentally, spiritually,
and emotionally
before you take on more.

Considering this season,

what are the top areas of my life that I need to focus on?

_____

_____

_____

_____

_____

_____

_____

_____

_____

_____

_____

_____

_____

_____

_____

_____

_____

_____

_____

_____

_____

_____

_____

_____

_____

_____

QUICK TIP:

Healing and growth is a process that isn't always linear. When you feel like life has put you two steps back, instead of asking yourself, "Why me?" ask yourself, "What do I need during this time?" Maybe it's more support, more information, resources, or direction. Whatever it may be, resist falling into a cycle of shame; instead, use this time to lean into what you need to build yourself back on a firm foundation. You're not failing; you're having a human experience.

TODAY I FEEL . . .

Boundaries are healthy
and often necessary
for personal growth
and healing.

How have I been doing with my time management lately?

What do I need to adjust going forward?

_____

_____

_____

_____

_____

_____

_____

_____

_____

_____

_____

_____

_____

_____

_____

QUICK TIP:

Think about managing your tasks not only around your time but around your *energy*. Is there a time of the day when you tend to feel more energetic and focused versus a time of day when you feel more lethargic or drained? This is common for many of us. So, to improve the flow in your day, consider scheduling your harder tasks that take more thinking power or creativity when you have the most energy in the day and those automatic or more "mindless" tasks during the times when you have less energy.

TODAY I'M GRATEFUL FOR . . .

God heals
in more ways
than one.
He is sovereign
enough to work
all things together
for good.

What matters most in life right now is . . .

_____
_____
_____
_____
_____
_____
_____
_____
_____
_____
_____
_____
_____
_____
_____
_____
_____
_____
_____
_____
_____
_____
_____
_____
_____
_____
_____

_____

_____

_____

_____

_____

_____

_____

_____

_____

_____

_____

_____

_____

_____

QUICK TIP:

How would your life look if you thought about it backwards? If you were to look back on your life, what would be the things you wish you did more of; who are the people you wish you spent more time with; what are the worries you wish you let go of; what are the demands you wish you didn't let take over your life? These are the things you need to start basing your life around now to lead a life that truly aligns with your convictions and values in the end. Consider thinking of your life backwards and see what you come up with.

MY PRAYER FOR TODAY IS . . .

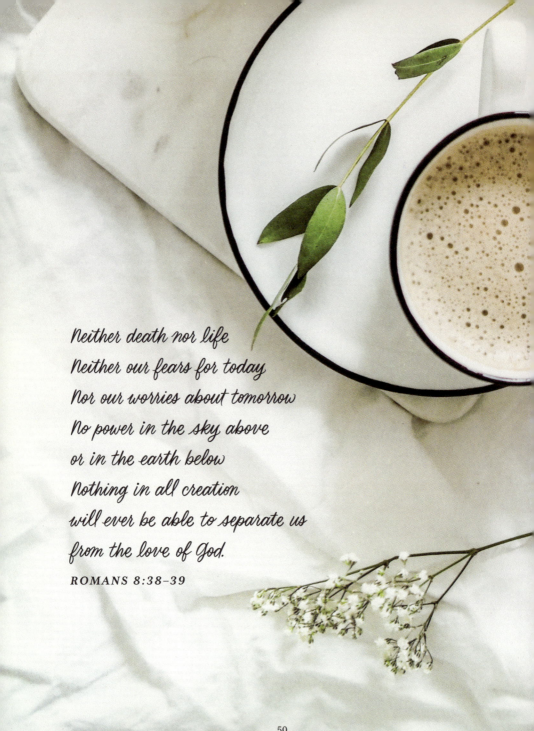

Neither death nor life
Neither our fears for today
Nor our worries about tomorrow
No power in the sky above
or in the earth below
Nothing in all creation
will ever be able to separate us
from the love of God.

ROMANS 8:38–39

If my mood were a color today,

what color would it be and why?

_____

_____

_____

_____

_____

_____

_____

_____

_____

_____

_____

_____

_____

_____

QUICK TIP:

Remember that emotions are signals, not the enemy. They're natural and intuitive God-given signs to reconnect you to your basic needs, convictions, and areas of healing. Choosing to be self-aware about our emotions doesn't mean we have to let our feelings rule us or define us, but they can lead us toward having more honest insight about ourselves. Wisdom and discernment—hand in hand with emotional indicators—can ultimately lead us to genuine growth.

TODAY I HOPE . . .

You are most empowered
in your calling by growing
in the way that God is
currently shaping you
according to your makeup
and purpose over your life.

What are the natural strengths I thrive from,

and what are some examples?

_____

_____

_____

_____

_____

_____

_____

_____

_____

_____

_____

_____

_____

_____

_____

QUICK TIP:

When you feel like you're being pulled into the comparison trap, consider reframing how you're seeing things. Instead of feeling discouragement or shame, understand that it's more than likely you've found traits about a person you either admire or want to grow in—and that's okay! Identify how you might want to grow in certain areas and what that could look like for you, or accept that it's something you admire, but it isn't for you—and release it.

TODAY I FEEL . . .

First things first:
let go of what
you can't control.

How have my sleep habits been lately?

What helps or doesn't help?

_____
_____
_____
_____
_____
_____
_____
_____
_____
_____
_____
_____
_____
_____
_____
_____
_____
_____
_____
_____
_____
_____
_____
_____
_____
_____
_____
_____

_____

_____

_____

_____

_____

_____

_____

_____

_____

_____

_____

_____

_____

_____

QUICK TIP:

Sleep is your body's most natural and powerful recovery system for both your brain and body. However, having trouble falling asleep and staying asleep is something that plagues too many people. Consider creating a regular nighttime routine that signals to your body that it's time to wind down. Whether that be turning off electronics an hour before bed to reduce sensory overload, using an eye mask, putting on a calming scent like lavender, or listening to a Scripture meditation, getting your body on an intentional cycle can be one of the best things you do for your overall well-being.

TODAY I'M GRATEFUL FOR . . .

How anxious am I feeling right now?

☐ 1 Slightly worried but functioning as usual   ☐ 2 Mildly growing fear and stress   ☐ 3 Can't focus and obsessive overthinking   ☐ 4 Losing control with physical discomfort   ☐ 5 Nearing anxiety attack

LET IT OUT: *What has happened or is about to happen that's causing my anxiety?*

_____

_____

_____

IDENTIFY: *Why does this scare me? What are my thoughts saying?*

_____

_____

_____

PERSPECTIVE CHANGE: *These are two other ways I could look at the situation . . .*

1. _____

_____

2. _____

_____

Stop. Breathe. Is this outside my control?

IF YES, I CAN NO LONGER CARRY THE BURDEN AND I RELEASE MYSELF FROM THE BONDAGE OF THAT WHICH I HAVE NO CONTROL.

This is the first step I can take to face the situation and overcome my fear:

_____

Who can I talk to or ask for prayer?

_____

Two things I am grateful for in this moment:

1. _____

2. _____

DATE: _____   62

My Goal Tracker

MY GOAL:

TO BE ACHIEVED BY:

The specific steps I need to take:

- [ ]
- [ ]
- [ ]
- [ ]
- [ ]

PRIORITY GOALS FOR THE WEEK	DATE COMPLETED

I'M REWARDING MYSELF FOR FULFILLING MY GOALS BY:

*Our thinking
may not always be perfect,
but at any time, we can
always realign ourselves
with the hope of God's truth.*

Three words that describe

this season of my life are . . . because . . .

_____
_____
_____
_____
_____
_____
_____
_____
_____
_____
_____
_____
_____
_____
_____
_____
_____
_____
_____
_____
_____
_____
_____
_____
_____
_____
_____

_____

_____

_____

_____

_____

_____

_____

_____

_____

_____

_____

_____

_____

_____

QUICK TIP:

Think about preventative mental care. Have you ever paused to note the pattern of signs when you notice your mental health worsening? Maybe you feel irritable, have problems sleeping, or start to feel disconnected from reality? Sometimes it's so easy to get sucked into the busyness of life and our thoughts that we don't realize how bad things have gotten until we're burned-out, deeply hopeless, or in severe mental distress. Identify the signs that your mental health may be declining so you can hold yourself accountable to get the support you need in the moment.

MY PRAYER FOR TODAY IS . . .

The same power that raised Christ from the grave lives in you.

ROMANS 8:11

What would my day look like

if I were more present?

_____
_____
_____
_____
_____
_____
_____
_____
_____
_____
_____
_____
_____
_____
_____
_____
_____
_____
_____
_____
_____
_____
_____
_____
_____
_____
_____
_____
_____

QUICK TIP:

Research has shown that our brains work best when we take a short break after ninety minutes of work or productivity, because that's when we start to lose steam. Consider breaking your day down into ninety-minute focus blocks with moments of mental rest in between so you can show up fully for your day. Whether it be focusing on a task, interacting with the person in front of you, or resting at home—wherever your attention is, let it be one hundred percent there. And as you drift off to sleep, you should feel more satisfied with your day.

TODAY I HOPE . . .

Having faith often means letting go of every fear, doubt, and uncertainty to understand one thing: God is faithful and He cares for you.

Who has been a big support to me lately, and

how can I do better about letting myself be seen and supported?

_____

_____

_____

_____

_____

_____

_____

_____

_____

_____

_____

_____

_____

_____

_____

QUICK TIP:

There's a difference between *perceived* support and *received* support. Perceived support is how much support we think we have from those around us. Received support is how much support we're *actually* experiencing from those around us. Knowing there may be people who are there for us and actually opening up and receiving that love and support in times of need are two different things. You are worthy of the latter. It doesn't mean you've failed. It doesn't disqualify you. It simply means you're human and worth the grace of feeling supported through the trials of this human experience.

TODAY I FEEL . . .

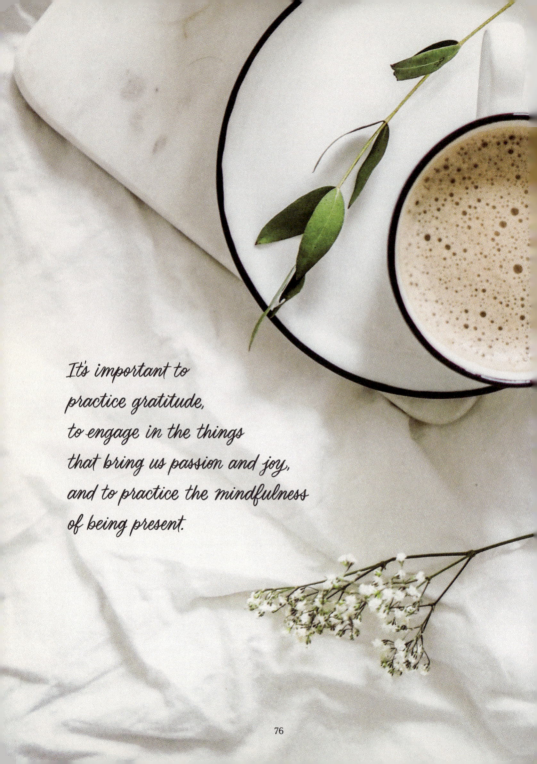

It's important to
practice gratitude,
to engage in the things
that bring us passion and joy,
and to practice the mindfulness
of being present.

What is a lesson learned that

I would have told myself a year ago?

_____
_____
_____
_____
_____
_____
_____
_____
_____
_____
_____
_____
_____
_____
_____
_____
_____
_____
_____
_____
_____
_____
_____
_____
_____
_____
_____

_____

_____

_____

_____

_____

_____

_____

_____

_____

_____

_____

_____

_____

_____

QUICK TIP:

Sometimes things break down so they can be rebuilt healthier than before. Breakdowns can lead to a new cycle of habits and new growth that you wouldn't have achieved otherwise. They can help you learn how to take care of yourself and reprioritize what matters most. When God allows the breaking, He is also in the rebuilding. Sometimes in healing and rebuilding, it feels like we're going backwards; but we're really being pulled back to be launched again farther than before—just like an arrow—farther than our previous mindsets and habits could take us.

TODAY I'M GRATEFUL FOR . . .

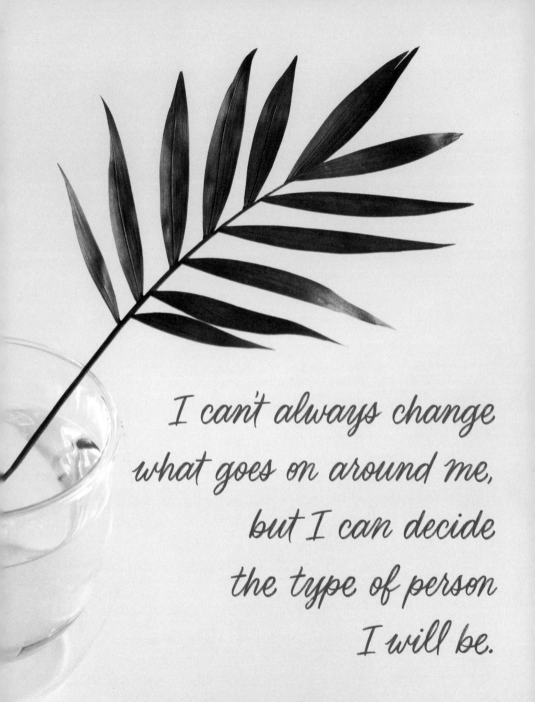

I can't always change
what goes on around me,
but I can decide
the type of person
I will be.

What are five principles I choose to live by

no matter what's happening in my life?

_____

_____

_____

_____

_____

_____

_____

_____

_____

_____

_____

_____

_____

QUICK TIP:

Core beliefs are the values and convictions we choose to guide our lives. The insecurity of cognitive dissonance takes place when our actions aren't aligning with how we believe we're supposed to live. When we understand and have clarity on the principles that guide our lives, it will impact how we interact in our relationships. Our attitudes and actions don't depend on the events or behaviors around us that we can't control; rather our core beliefs anchor us in the integrity of who God has called us to be. This is grounded living.

MY PRAYER FOR TODAY IS . . .

Give yourself permission
to practice the pause.
Still yourself,
breathe deeply, and
hush before God.

Describe four things I see, three things I feel,

two things I hear, and one thing I taste.

_____

_____

_____

_____

_____

_____

_____

_____

_____

_____

_____

_____

_____

_____

_____

_____

_____

_____

_____

_____

_____

_____

_____

_____

_____

_____

_____

QUICK TIP:

When you feel overwhelmed, you can use this grounding practice to reconnect with your senses and help regulate your nervous system. Practice humming or rubbing behind your earlobes to stimulate your vagus nerve. The vagus nerve is the longest cranial nerve in your body and largely makes up the nerves of your parasympathetic nervous system—also known as rest and digest, in contrast to our fight or flight mode—bringing your body back to a calm state.

TODAY I HOPE . . .

Jesus said, "Come to Me,
all of you who are weary
and carry heavy burdens,
and I will give you rest."

MATTHEW 11:28 NLT

When I feel triggered by anxiety or overwhelmed,

I choose to . . .

_____

_____

_____

_____

_____

_____

_____

_____

_____

_____

_____

_____

_____

_____

QUICK TIP:

Being proactive versus reactive toward our mental health means having a plan for how to respond when we feel triggered. A simple practice is identifying your ABCs. A is the Activating event (that triggered you). B is the automatic Belief your thoughts created from the trigger. And C is the Consequence of how you reacted from this trigger. Notice your ABCs to become more self-aware of your triggers, but also consider two healthy ways you'll choose to respond (instead of react) should it come up again.

TODAY I FEEL . . .

My Self-Therapy Anxiety Guide
A PRACTICAL JOURNALING GUIDE TO UNTWISTING ANXIETY

How anxious am I feeling right now?

☐ **1** Slightly worried but functioning as usual

☐ **2** Mildly growing fear and stress

☐ **3** Can't focus and obsessive overthinking

☐ **4** Losing control with physical discomfort

☐ **5** Nearing anxiety attack

LET IT OUT: *What has happened or is about to happen that's causing my anxiety?*

_____

_____

_____

IDENTIFY: *Why does this scare me? What are my thoughts saying?*

_____

_____

_____

PERSPECTIVE CHANGE: *These are two other ways I could look at the situation . . .*

1. _____

_____

2. _____

_____

Stop. Breathe. Is this outside my control?
IF YES, I CAN NO LONGER CARRY THE BURDEN AND I RELEASE MYSELF FROM THE BONDAGE OF THAT WHICH I HAVE NO CONTROL.

This is the first step I can take to face the situation and overcome my fear:

_____

Who can I talk to or ask for prayer?

_____

Two things I am grateful for in this moment:

1. _____

2. _____

DATE:_____   92

My Goal Tracker

MY GOAL:

TO BE ACHIEVED BY:

The specific steps I need to take:

☐

☐

☐

☐

☐

PRIORITY GOALS FOR THE WEEK	DATE COMPLETED

I'M REWARDING MYSELF FOR FULFILLING MY GOALS BY:

DATE:

God is not surprised by your thoughts and feelings. Today He meets you right where you are.

Describe yourself in ten words.

What would they be and why?

_____

_____

_____

_____

_____

_____

_____

_____

_____

_____

_____

_____

_____

_____

QUICK TIP:

We often find there is a gap between our *real self* and our *ideal self* as we grow through this life. Our real self is who we really are in this present moment. Our ideal self is the type of person we aspire to be, and this self-image can change and evolve. Today, be reminded that while it's okay to be forward-thinking, there is also value in where you are and how far you've come. Don't forget to pause and find gratitude in what you've already achieved and the things that already surround you. Rest and be content in this. You've been growing all along.

TODAY I'M GRATEFUL FOR . . .

Even when
I am slipping,
Your unfailing
love holds me up!

PSALM 94:18

What is one thing I feel convicted about

changing in my life right now? Why?

_____

_____

_____

_____

_____

_____

_____

_____

_____

_____

_____

_____

_____

_____

QUICK TIP:

Habit-stacking can be a great way to seamlessly develop a new pattern of healthy habits. By pairing the new habit with something that's already a part of your daily routine, this makes the consistency more achievable. For example, if you want to start journaling or reading more, pair it with your morning cup of coffee. If you want to drink more water, pair having a glass of water with brushing your teeth. What new desired habits can you stack with already existing ones in your routine?

MY PRAYER FOR TODAY IS . . .

In waves of
overwhelming emotions,
God is our anchor.
Nothing can take you
out of His hands.

What personal needs am I neglecting right now?

How can I change this?

_____

_____

_____

_____

_____

_____

_____

_____

_____

_____

_____

_____

_____

_____

_____

_____

_____

_____

_____

_____

_____

_____

_____

_____

_____

_____

_____

_____

_____

_____

_____

_____

_____

_____

_____

_____

_____

_____

_____

QUICK TIP:

According to Dr. Saundra Dalton-Smith's theory of rest, there are different types of rest that can help prevent burnout. For example: 1) Physical rest and the time your body needs to relax and recover. 2) Mental rest and taking a break from tasks that take strenuous mental power. 3) Social rest and being around life-giving people who you can fully be yourself around. 4) Sensory rest and taking a break from screen time or anything that overloads your senses. 5) Emotional rest and taking space from things that weigh heavily on your emotions. 6) Creative rest like taking a walk outside or surrounding yourself with things that fuel your inspiration. 7) Spiritual rest, which is really leaning in to the things that refill your soul like prayer, worship, or Scripture reading. What type of rest do you need these days?

TODAY I HOPE . . .

Consider this:
God loves you
because He wants
to love you.

What is the best advice or quote I've heard recently,

and how does it apply to my life?

_____

_____

_____

_____

_____

_____

_____

_____

_____

_____

_____

_____

_____

_____

QUICK TIP:

Romans 8:28 reminds us that God works for the good of those who love Him, who have been called according to His purpose. When we aren't exactly clear on which direction to take or how to apply the advice we're given, know that it's okay to both pray for confirmation and use practical wisdom and discernment. Make a list of the pros and cons, weigh the outcome, consider trusted wisdom, and know that God is with you in either path you take. Either way, He has good plans for you!

TODAY I FEEL . . .

Taking care of our mental health means being both prayerful and practical.

Three things that help me feel alive are . . .

_____
_____
_____
_____
_____
_____
_____
_____
_____
_____
_____
_____
_____
_____
_____
_____
_____
_____
_____
_____
_____
_____
_____
_____
_____
_____
_____
_____
_____

_____

_____

_____

_____

_____

_____

_____

_____

_____

_____

_____

_____

_____

_____

QUICK TIP:

Pay attention to the types of things, events, and activities that quickly drain you versus the things that naturally make your mind and soul come alive. It's no accident that these may be the very things that point toward your strengths, your passion, and your disposition. Decide how you can minimize your interaction with soul-drainers and maximize it with soul-fillers.

TODAY I'M GRATEFUL FOR . . .

Even on
the hardest days,
we still have
the greatest God.

What does giving and receiving love

look like practically in your life right now?

_____

_____

_____

_____

_____

_____

_____

_____

_____

_____

_____

_____

QUICK TIP:

Do you know what your love language is? Because of our different personalities, experiences, and upbringings, many of us have different ways in which we translate how we feel most loved. Whether it be through words of affirmation, acts of service, receiving gifts, quality time, or physical touch, knowing our love language and being able to share this with others can help our relationships feel more understanding and fulfilling. Check out the work of Gary Chapman in _The 5 Love Languages_, and take the quiz to learn your love language at www.5lovelanguages.com.

MY PRAYER FOR TODAY IS . . .

Your Heavenly Father is and always will be the beginning and the end. As you cling to Him each step of the way, may your faith rise above your doubts.

Describe three things I enjoyed doing

this month and want to continue.

_____

_____

_____

_____

_____

_____

_____

_____

_____

_____

_____

_____

_____

_____

_____

_____

_____

_____

_____

_____

_____

_____

_____

_____

QUICK TIP:

As we take care of our mental health, we can rely on some level on our intuitive wisdom. This means simply paying attention to what is or isn't working in our lives. Take a step back and notice which things elevate and improve your mental health when you make space for them in your life. Try to make it a priority to include more of these things on a regular basis. Notice which activities in your life tend to weaken your mental health and consider creating better boundaries around these things. What changes do you need to make in your life for your overall mental well-being?

TODAY I HOPE . . .

My Self-Therapy Anxiety Guide
A PRACTICAL JOURNALING GUIDE TO UNTWISTING ANXIETY

How anxious am I feeling right now?

☐ 1 Slightly worried but functioning as usual

☐ 2 Mildly growing fear and stress

☐ 3 Can't focus and obsessive overthinking

☐ 4 Losing control with physical discomfort

☐ 5 Nearing anxiety attack

LET IT OUT: *What has happened or is about to happen that's causing my anxiety?*

_____

_____

_____

IDENTIFY: *Why does this scare me? What are my thoughts saying?*

_____

_____

_____

PERSPECTIVE CHANGE: *These are two other ways I could look at the situation . . .*

1. _____

_____

2. _____

_____

Stop. Breathe. Is this outside my control?

IF YES, I CAN NO LONGER CARRY THE BURDEN AND I RELEASE MYSELF FROM THE BONDAGE OF THAT WHICH I HAVE NO CONTROL.

This is the first step I can take to face the situation and overcome my fear:

_____

Who can I talk to or ask for prayer?

_____

Two things I am grateful for in this moment:

1. _____

2. _____

DATE: _____   122

My Goal Tracker

FOR THE WEEK OF:

MY GOAL:

TO BE ACHIEVED BY:

The specific steps I need to take:

- [ ]
- [ ]
- [ ]
- [ ]
- [ ]

PRIORITY GOALS FOR THE WEEK	DATE COMPLETED

I'M REWARDING MYSELF FOR FULFILLING MY GOALS BY:

DATE:

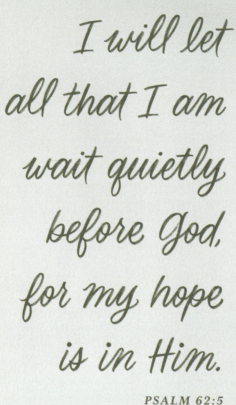

I will let all that I am wait quietly before God, for my hope is in Him.

PSALM 62:5

Has my anxiety gotten better or worse this month,

and what do I think has contributed to this?

_____

_____

_____

_____

_____

_____

_____

_____

_____

_____

_____

_____

_____

_____

_____

_____

_____

_____

_____

_____

_____

_____

_____

_____

_____

_____

_____

_____

_____

_____

_____

_____

_____

_____

_____

_____

_____

QUICK TIP:

Magnification is a cognitive bias when we enlarge an issue in our lives and it soon takes over our minds from being able to see any other perspective. This is commonly the case with anxiety. While our fears may feel valid, be reminded that fear isn't all there is to your life. Breathe and remember the moments, the parts of life, and the relationships that have felt meaningful or brought you joy, and continue to seek these moments. But if the mental distress becomes too much to manage, there is no shame in finding support and gaining some helpful tools from a counselor or therapist. You are worthy of freedom and finding some relief.

TODAY I FEEL . . .

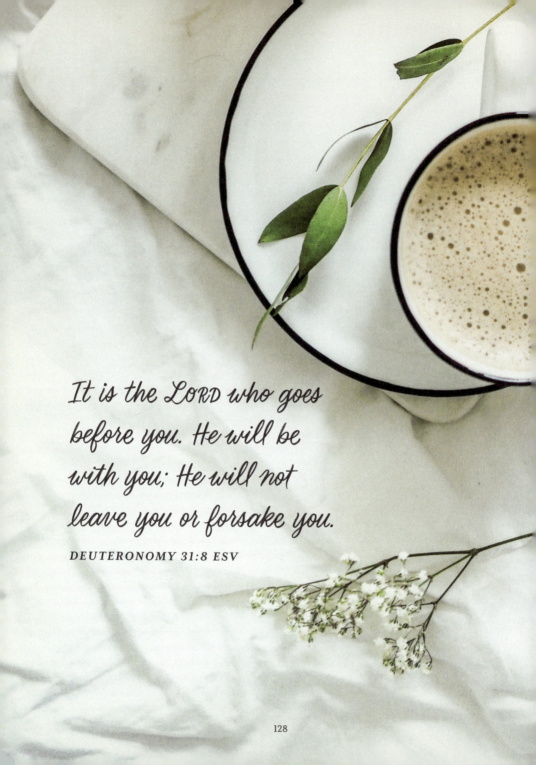

It is the LORD who goes before you. He will be with you; He will not leave you or forsake you.

DEUTERONOMY 31:8 ESV

Write about an experience

that changed your outlook on life.

_____

_____

_____

_____

_____

_____

_____

_____

_____

_____

_____

_____

_____

_____

_____

_____

_____

_____

_____

_____

_____

_____

_____

_____

_____

_____

_____

_____

_____

_____

_____

_____

_____

_____

_____

_____

_____

_____

_____

_____

_____

_____

_____

QUICK TIP:

Dehydration can slow down brain function, cognition, attention, and focus. Water is literally lubricant for your organs; this includes your brain, which is made up of about 75% water. Consider what it may look like for you to stay hydrated throughout the day, such as keeping a water bottle by your bed or on your desk.

TODAY I'M GRATEFUL FOR . . .

*God is my refuge
and strength, always
ready to help me
in times of trouble.*

PSALM 46:1

Describe your own personal thoughts or beliefs

regarding an event that happened in the news or media this week.

_____

_____

_____

_____

_____

_____

_____

_____

_____

_____

_____

_____

_____

_____

_____

_____

_____

_____

_____

_____

_____

_____

_____

_____

_____

_____

_____

_____

_____

_____

_____

_____

_____

_____

_____

_____

_____

_____

_____

_____

_____

QUICK TIP:

You are a separate individual with your own individual thoughts and emotions. Allow yourself the in-between space for your own process. You can make a conscious choice, differentiating which thoughts and emotions belong to you and which belong to others—especially in an age of social media where we pick up an overwhelming amount of information before we have time to process it. Remember that it's okay to practice the pause, check in with yourself and your convictions, and give yourself permission to personally process before responding to or taking on a matter.

MY PRAYER FOR TODAY IS . . .

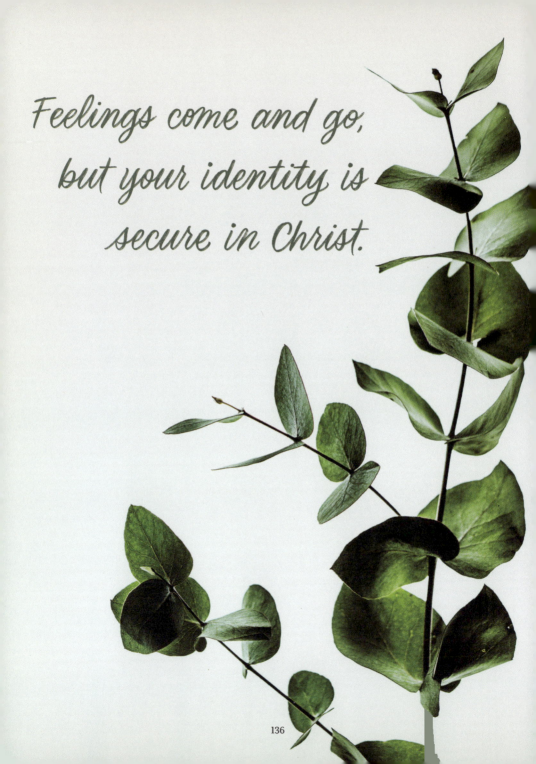

Feelings come and go,
but your identity is
secure in Christ.

On a scale of 1–10, my mental health

is at a . . . today because . . .

_____

_____

_____

_____

_____

_____

_____

_____

_____

_____

_____

_____

_____

_____

_____

_____

_____

_____

_____

_____

_____

_____

_____

_____

_____

_____

_____

_____

_____

_____

_____

_____

_____

_____

_____

_____

_____

_____

_____

_____

_____

_____

_____

_____

QUICK TIP:

Do you sit inside most of the day glued to your screen? Due to the development of modern-day technology, many people work indoors and are less likely to labor in the sun. This means that we may be missing out on the essential nutrients that sunlight helps synthesize in our bodies like vitamin D, which plays a role in the production of serotonin (a neurochemical that regulates our mood). In fact, low levels of serotonin and a lack of vitamin D have been associated with depression and anxiety. That being said, stretch out your body, step outside to get some fresh air, and soak in some vitamin D today!

TODAY I HOPE . . .

The Word of God
is our spiritual mirror.
It reflects who
we were created to be
despite how we feel
about ourselves.

Write about an area of your life where you need
to create better boundaries for your own health.

_____
_____
_____
_____
_____
_____
_____
_____
_____
_____
_____
_____
_____
_____
_____
_____
_____
_____
_____
_____
_____
_____
_____
_____
_____
_____

_____

_____

_____

_____

_____

_____

_____

_____

_____

_____

_____

_____

_____

_____

QUICK TIP:

You can hear what a person is saying or what social media is projecting, but it doesn't mean you automatically have to take on that same mentality, especially if it puts your own mental health at risk. And if what you're hearing is anxiety-provoking or negative, it's already planted a seed in your emotions. This is why emotional boundaries are important. You can't always predict how the day will go, but you can choose to create a moment of space and take back ownership of your mind and emotions. Before the day begins, think about what you're allowing into your mind, and put appropriate boundaries in place to protect your mental health.

TODAY I FEEL . . .

Faith is not denying
mental or emotional hardship.
Faith is leaning in with honesty and
trusting that God meets us there.

Write about a defining event that changed the course of your life and how it has impacted the person you've become.

_____

_____

_____

_____

_____

_____

_____

_____

_____

_____

_____

_____

_____

_____

QUICK TIP:

If you're ruminating from a place of worry, most of the perspective you're acquiring is painted by fear. Identify and mentally release the parts that you have no control over to God. Consider visualizing this process by making a physical list of what they are. Then get realistic and deal with the things that you do have the ability to impact. But just start with what you can manage within the first twenty-four hours.

TODAY I'M GRATEFUL FOR . . .

If you're responding
to things much
differently—better—
than you would have
in the past,
you're growing.

148

What are some ways your upbringing

may have shaped who you are today?

_____

_____

_____

_____

_____

_____

_____

_____

_____

_____

_____

_____

_____

_____

QUICK TIP:

Sometimes we unknowingly live by limiting beliefs because we've never seen something done in our immediate family or our environment. This can cause us to repeat the limiting cycle or not expect anything better for ourselves. But you are worthy of breaking old cycles and creating something new even if you've never seen it done before. It's important to identify the automatic beliefs you have learned from your environment and experiences. This could mean participating in therapy or learning workshops or surrounding yourself with those who have already done the work and can show you what's possible. What have you decided will end and begin with you?

MY PRAYER FOR TODAY IS . . .

How anxious am I feeling right now?

☐ 1 Slightly worried but functioning as usual

☐ 2 Mildly growing fear and stress

☐ 3 Can't focus and obsessive overthinking

☐ 4 Losing control with physical discomfort

☐ 5 Nearing anxiety attack

LET IT OUT: *What has happened or is about to happen that's causing my anxiety?*

_____

_____

_____

IDENTIFY: *Why does this scare me? What are my thoughts saying?*

_____

_____

_____

PERSPECTIVE CHANGE: *These are two other ways I could look at the situation . . .*

1. _____

_____

2. _____

_____

Stop. Breathe. Is this outside my control?

IF YES, I CAN NO LONGER CARRY THE BURDEN AND I RELEASE MYSELF FROM THE BONDAGE OF THAT WHICH I HAVE NO CONTROL.

This is the first step I can take to face the situation and overcome my fear:

_____

Who can I talk to or ask for prayer?

_____

Two things I am grateful for in this moment:

1. _____

2. _____

DATE:_____   152

My Goal Tracker

MY GOAL:

_____

_____

TO BE ACHIEVED BY:

_____

The specific steps I need to take:

☐ _____

☐ _____

☐ _____

☐ _____

☐ _____

PRIORITY GOALS FOR THE WEEK	DATE COMPLETED

I'M REWARDING MYSELF FOR FULFILLING MY GOALS BY:

_____

153   DATE:_____

If God renews His mercies
upon you each day
(Lamentations 3:22–23),
surely you can spare
some for yourself.

Ten things that bring me joy are . . .

_____

_____

_____

_____

_____

_____

_____

_____

_____

_____

_____

_____

_____

_____

QUICK TIP:

Identify any self-sabotaging beliefs you may have developed around living in the fullness of joy. Sometimes we won't allow ourselves to get too happy, enjoy ourselves too much, or experience the fullness of a relationship all because we fear disappointment. But making these assumptions causes us to go into situations from a place of fear and disappointment—we expect it before it even happens! However, God has called you to life and life abundantly, and He's got you—no matter the outcome. Joy comes from the Lord, so let it fill you up when it comes, and don't resist it.

TODAY I HOPE . . .

It's okay to start
with each day and
take it one moment
at a time.

What are three emotions I am currently feeling, and

what reasons do I think have contributed to these emotions?

_____
_____
_____
_____
_____
_____
_____
_____
_____
_____
_____
_____
_____
_____
_____

QUICK TIP:

Movement and exercise are two of the most beneficial and natural forms of self-therapy to manage anxiety and depression. Neuroscience has shown that when we are proactive and engage in any level of exercise, endorphins and adrenaline are released into the brain, giving our mood an instant pick-me-up (sometimes known as a "runner's high")! Physical activity also circulates your energy and promotes mental resilience to help you push past what you feel. Find a form of movement that suits you, even if it's moderate, for around thirty minutes in your day.

TODAY I FEEL . . .

God uses people to help heal people.

Who is someone

you currently look up to and why?

_____

_____

_____

_____

_____

_____

_____

_____

_____

_____

_____

_____

_____

_____

_____

_____

_____

_____

_____

_____

_____

_____

_____

_____

_____

_____

_____

_____

_____

_____

_____

_____

_____

_____

_____

_____

_____

_____

_____

_____

_____

_____

QUICK TIP:

Whose voices subtly play a role in your thoughts, opinions, and choices? And more importantly, what is the fruit of that? Jesus says that you'll know a tree by its fruit—by what they produce in your life. You can't always choose who's around you, but you can choose who you surround yourself with and whose words you decide to give weight to. Identify those voices currently in your life, get as clear as you can, reflect on the fruit they bear in your life. And remember, thriving happens in the wise and supportive relationships that propel us into all that God created us to be.

TODAY I'M GRATEFUL FOR . . .

*God is for you. . . .
even when it feels like
your thoughts are
against you.*

Write about an area of your life

you need more support in right now.

_____
_____
_____
_____
_____
_____
_____
_____
_____
_____
_____
_____
_____
_____
_____
_____
_____
_____
_____
_____
_____
_____
_____
_____
_____
_____
_____
_____

_____

_____

_____

_____

_____

_____

_____

_____

_____

_____

_____

_____

_____

_____

QUICK TIP:

Ask yourself less about what's *doable* and more about what's *sustainable* for your soul, for your mind, and for your body. Hold a space of grace and rest for yourself when you get easily caught up in the striving, the proving, the frustration for lack of results, and the burnout in a culture that expects nonstop production. Your worth was never tied to how you show up for the rest of the world; it was always in your *being*. The world will keep going, but there is only one of you. So, take care of yourself.

MY PRAYER FOR TODAY IS . . .

By taking the time
to pause and reflect,
we can expand our gaze
on the bigger picture that
God has in place for us.

Write about the biggest lesson you've learned

from the life of someone who has passed away.

_____

_____

_____

_____

_____

_____

_____

_____

_____

_____

_____

_____

_____

_____

QUICK TIP:

The primary purpose of words is not just communication but creation. Words create. Words shape our culture and our attitudes. Words can tear down, or they can build up. Words can be reckless or intentional. What is the environment you're creating with your words lately? Choose to be led by faith in the way that you speak to yourself. Choose to be led by words of growth and healing. We can't control the messages around us, but we can choose our words. Choose intentionally today.

TODAY I HOPE . . .

It's so easy to define
ourselves by the ups
and downs of our days.
But the truth is, we are
who He says we are
in spite of how we feel:
wholeheartedly loved . . .
eternally secure . . .
wonderfully made . . .
called and set apart
for a purpose.
No. Matter. What.

When I look in the mirror

I see a woman/man who is . . .

175

_____

_____

_____

_____

_____

_____

_____

_____

_____

_____

_____

_____

_____

_____

_____

QUICK TIP:

You may find it beneficial for you to have an affirmational verse or phrase for each day that you stick somewhere in sight and draw back to throughout the day. For example, you could post a verse on your bathroom mirror or office desk or computer. Here are some of my go-to affirmations: "When I am afraid, I put my trust in You" (Psalm 56:3 NIV); I have been called to peace (Colossians 3:15); I will "let all that I am wait quietly before God, for my hope is in Him" (Psalm 62:5 NLT). Find your meditative affirmations or anchor verses to revisit throughout the day.

TODAY I FEEL . . .

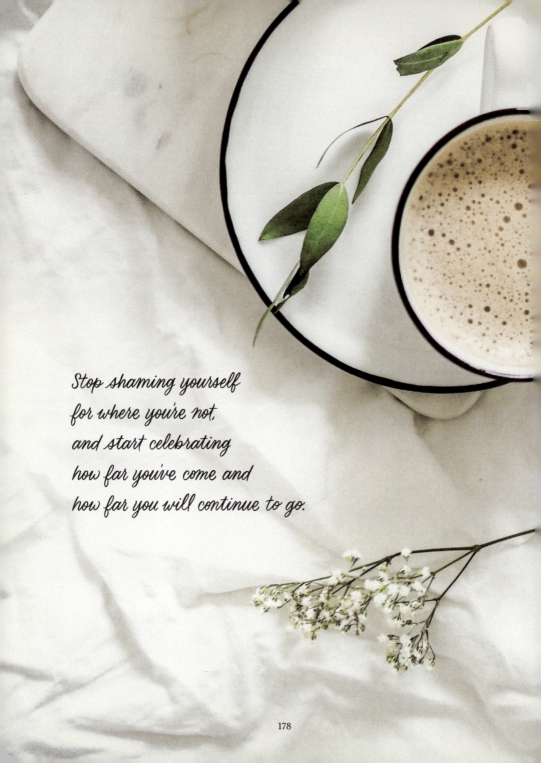

Stop shaming yourself
for where you're not,
and start celebrating
how far you've come and
how far you will continue to go.

Write about a favorite childhood memory.

_____

_____

_____

_____

_____

_____

_____

_____

_____

_____

_____

_____

_____

QUICK TIP:

Mood congruent memory is when our brains access memories aligned with the current mood we're in. Research has shown that our present mood has a strong influence on the type of memories we more easily recall at any given moment. When we're anxious, we more easily recall our fears. When we feel discouraged, we more easily recall our disappointments in life. Sometimes breaking this cycle can be as simple as shifting our thinking to other events or perspectives that contradict our current feeling. Before you define your entire life by a single moment, remember that these biases exist and can influence your mood.

TODAY I'M GRATEFUL FOR . . .

My Self-Therapy Anxiety Guide
A PRACTICAL JOURNALING GUIDE TO UNTWISTING ANXIETY

How anxious am I feeling right now?

☐ 1 Slightly worried but functioning as usual

☐ 2 Mildly growing fear and stress

☐ 3 Can't focus and obsessive overthinking

☐ 4 Losing control with physical discomfort

☐ 5 Nearing anxiety attack

LET IT OUT: *What has happened or is about to happen that's causing my anxiety?*

_____

_____

IDENTIFY: *Why does this scare me? What are my thoughts saying?*

_____

_____

PERSPECTIVE CHANGE: *These are two other ways I could look at the situation . . .*

1. _____

_____

2. _____

_____

Stop. Breathe. Is this outside my control?

IF YES, I CAN NO LONGER CARRY THE BURDEN AND I RELEASE MYSELF FROM THE BONDAGE OF THAT WHICH I HAVE NO CONTROL.

This is the first step I can take to face the situation and overcome my fear:

_____

Who can I talk to or ask for prayer?

_____

Two things I am grateful for in this moment:

1. _____

2. _____

DATE:_____   182

My Goal Tracker

MY GOAL:

TO BE ACHIEVED BY:

The specific steps I need to take:

☐

☐

☐

☐

☐

PRIORITY GOALS FOR THE WEEK	DATE COMPLETED

I'M REWARDING MYSELF FOR FULFILLING MY GOALS BY:

DATE:

God's grace begins afresh each day. Give yourself the grace to start over tomorrow too.

If I had the ability to change one thing in the world,

I'd hope to change . . .

QUICK TIP:

Overthinking goes hand in hand with control issues—the burden of having to know everything, to figure it all out, to have all the answers. When you can't focus because your mind is running on and on about something that doesn't pertain to the moment you're in, designate a better time to think it through. Literally plan for a time to journal or consider it later, and decide until then to let it go. You'll feel better because you can redirect your focus to what's in front of you without the lingering feeling that things have gone unresolved. Remember, God has not given you a spirit of fear but of power and a sound mind (II Timothy 1:7). Let it go, and rest in Him.

MY PRAYER FOR TODAY IS . . .

The LORD will fulfill
His purpose for me.

PSALM 138:8 ESV

When do you feel most at peace?

QUICK TIP:

Don't forget to stretch and release today. It's known that people with chronic anxiety tend to clench their jaw and tighten their muscles which can create accumulated tension in the body. What a wonderful idea it would be to set aside a time, possibly in the morning, just to engage in some stretching exercises. And when you're doing this, while focusing on the flow of your body and breath, give thanks to God for your body and for the day He's made, and continue to either mentally or verbally give thanks or recite Scripture.

WHAT I'VE LEARNED ABOUT MYSELF THROUGH THIS JOURNALING EXPERIENCE:

_____

_____

_____

_____

_____

_____

_____

_____

_____

_____

_____

_____

_____

_____

_____

_____

_____

_____

_____

_____

_____

_____

_____

_____

_____

_____

Known: An Inspirational Journal for Self-Discovery
© 2023 Brittney Moses. All rights reserved.
First Edition, July 2023

Published by:

21154 Highway 16 East
Siloam Springs, AR 72761
dayspring.com

A few select verses are author paraphrased.
Written by: Brittney Moses
Cover Design by: Jessica Wei

Printed in China
Prime: J9607
ISBN: 978-1-64870-927-2